Four ways of dealing with bullies

To Shawn Butala —

With greatest admiration,
respect, and affection.

Hugs,

Richard Steen

March 26. 2001

Four ways of dealing with bullies

Poems by Richard Lemm

Wolsak and Wynn . Toronto

Typeset in Garamond, printed in Canada by
The Coach House Printing Company, Toronto.

Front cover art: *The Great Weight* © Stephen MacInnis
Cover design: The Coach House Printing Company
Author's photograph: Tom MacDonald

Several of these poems have appeared in *Arc, Cormorant, Event, The Fiddlehead, The Malahat Review, The New Quarterly, Pottersfield Portfolio,* and *Proserpine.* "Sandlot" was broadcast on CBC's "Morningside" and "Sunday Morning," and published in Peter Gzowski's *The Fourth Morningside Papers* (McClelland & Stewart, 1991). "At Skeleton Lake" and "Stone Heart" were published in *Border Lines: Contemporary Poems in English* (Copp Clark, 1995). "Metamorphosis" was published in *Vintage 97-98* (Quarry Press, 1998). Several poems were broadcast on CBC Radio's "Maritime Magazine."

The publisher gratefully acknowledges the Canada Council for the Arts and the Ontario Arts Council for their generous support.

Wolsak and Wynn Publishers Ltd.
Post Office Box 316
Don Mills, Ontario, Canada M3C 2S7

Canadian Cataloguing in Publication Data

Lemm, Richard, 1946-
  Four ways of dealing with bullies

Poems.
ISBN 0-919897-75-4

I. Title.

PS8573.E547F68 2000   C811'.54   C00-930596-3
PR9199.3.L45F68 2000

For Lesley

CONTENTS

I
GILLETTE TIME

METAMORPHOSIS

In their bridal-white feathers the egrets
glide down to this Cuban beach,
their stately pose,
then lurch along the sand like Judy
McElroy in her elementary ballet
of polio braces across the minefield
at school, each step could detonate
ridicule, four-legged, cripple,
duck-walking, spastic. She was truly
what they call in warfare a hero
straight through enemy fire, without cover,
backup, or flinching, that same grim smile
that said (if it had been me), please
God, just let me reach the classroom
one more time without cracking, and falling
through those cracks to a dungeon where
I weep endlessly, rats begin to eat me alive, I am almost
a casualty, saved by the king's good
son, and they all
take my place in the rats' gnawing.

One morning we hide, snipers
behind a portable. Mick has brought
grenades, their thin
white shells, yolks
of flightless birds.
This is not me, but my hands
reach out, must have what Mick
passes around for protection
against the taunts that refusal would bring,
would contaminate me with Judy.
You can hear her coming, Meccano woman
clicking, scuffling. You can see us
leap out, shrieking baboons,
two or three of us hanging back, missiles
dropped or thrown wide of the mark,
but Judy is too cauled in egg white
and misery, twisting like a broken
windmill with her canes,
too robbed of whatever
kept her going, to notice any faces
peeled back to shame.
Why is it we rarely remember

what happens next? How Judy
made her exit, what cartoons
our separate minds played
at our first period desks.
Or if she watched from the classroom
windows our lunch-hour craving
to lunge and leap at baseballs,
each other. And with what
in her eyes. The tourists get too close
with their cameras, and the egret
extends its neck, unfolds its wings,
lifts away from our focusing.

FEAR

I am afraid of admitting
my fears. Except the most
undeniable: swimming in water
over my head; teaching a class
unprepared because my in-laws
kept me up half the night
with Peach Schnapps and crokinole;
or that nightmare recurring where
I kill someone with great pleasure.

Ten years old, I and Allan Ricci,
best friend and neighbour, love
the smell of gasoline, fill our
Boy Scout canteens from the hose
by the pumps at the Texaco.
(Later, we'd take extra long in
the finishing room of woodworking class.
O varnish, stain, and shellac.)

Allan's father keeps a can of white
gas in his garage, by the outboard motor.
No more three-block walks to the pumps.
No more descents to my basement and the
disappointment of linseed oil, the cheap
thrill of turpentine.
We were now disciples of
Mr Ricci, how he sniffed
a new bottle of olive oil, his brother's wine.

Mid-July, three straight days, patrons
of Chez Garage, we are connoisseurs of
cabernet hydrocarbons, the nose
and bouquet overpowering
all other functions in the brain.
Day four. Vaporous blue sky, heat
shimmering off the asphalt shingles of
Ricci's garage. Allan goes
for lunch, I sneak back, inhale,
sit on the cool concrete floor, lean
against the outboard motor, fall asleep.

Allan stands above me. "My mom says,
if you sniff gas then go out in the sun
you'll explode." He leaves.
Minutes pass. The sun is still
out there, streaming dangerously
through a window, reflecting off tools, ladders.
Hours pass. Angles of light
change, I move, carefully, as if
strapped with dynamite.

Meanwhile the heat
shrink-wraps the garage,
an incubator for the gas can.
Mr Ricci's ten-foot aluminium boat
is the best place to hide behind, especially
when his Buick comes up the driveway and
pulls inside. He is singing
"Fly Me to the Moon." The garage door closes.

My grandmother calls me for dinner.
Calls again, angry. Then
frantic, with my grandfather
sending my name like a carrier pigeon
through the yards, into the slanting
evening light, my name a magic
incantation to bury the sun.

The window purples. With dusk comes
silence, and my grandparents must be
inside with their anger, their
worry I don't think about, I am
only relieved that the sun won't burst
my gas-bloated body. I slide open
the door. And what slams

in my face is not whatever my grandparents
asked, said, or swore, but my fear of
telling that I was afraid
of blowing up, that I cowered,
even though I saved them from the grief of
my funeral, and spared Mr Ricci from
guilt over leaving white gas around.

FURNACE

The age of coal lingers in our basement
rattling down the chute
scooped and tumbling from the pages
of Dickens, the fireman's shove
on a stern wheeler leaving St Louis.

Descending to the underworld, Grandfather
Vulcan with thick gloves
and poker, face Apache
in the blistering glow, earth's
core, downcast souls, burning.

Then, one Easter Sunday, all pickaxe
and spade, we are lawn wreckers
about to loot China, Grandfather solemnly
blissful. We root
ourselves under Grandmother's irises

back-porch gaze and lemonade hands.
We are under the tulips' brains
and diving. Bones appear: Christmas
roast, Helga the German
witch's poisoned son, fragments of

caveman skull. We go deep
enough for death, so neighbours
home from church joke about gold
and swimming pools for leprechauns.
No. Footings of an anti-aircraft gun

pharaoh's tomb encircled by pyramids
a silver chalice traded for
centuries around the world and buried
here. I'm in school
when the oil tank rolls off the truck

to its pit, the old furnace broken
apart, the new one tuned
to hum soothingly. We shovel back dirt
sweep out the coal room, adapt
evolve, dialling with ease, the sun.

HOLIDAYS AND UNCLE CURT

1   Thanksgiving

The new moon that scar
on your cheek, more exotic than a rapier's
signature: a hundred-legged
centipede on a South Pacific island
bit your face, thinned you to rice
paper with fever. A US Navy 'Seabee'
building airstrips, diving into shelters
when the Japanese bombed and strafed,
then an insect nearly killed you.

Weeks of Hawaiian nurses who loved
the way you grinned and patted
your belly after meals. In post-war home
movies, your shining friends
and you smile eternally, jitterbug
with a frenzy in my wildest days
I've never known, and gulp
the liquor down. The men drape
arms around each other's shoulders and
veteran luck, flesh intact,
lives unclenched. Women spin,
cast out arms' length from their partners
reeling them in, squeezing so tight
the old film almost melts
from the heat, adoration, and wedding
plans that flicker
long after the projector cools.

2   Christmas Eve

My mother and father are not among
your movies' celebrants. They danced
before the war and his letters
from North Africa and Normandy, saved
with snapshots in a shoebox. One of her
handstand on his shoulders: turned
upside-down, she stands astonished
on the sky. Or Harvey lighting her
cigarette, that pleasure still burning
five decades beyond his death.
You and I nag her to quit.

We handle the heirloom ornaments
preciously, as if each broken globe
brings another death, beginning
with my father, smashed in a drunken
army buddy's car, followed by your father's
airplane into the sea, my mother too
shattered ever after to help
hang the snowflakes and tinsel,
though she smiles when you plug in
the lights blinking red and green like wingtips of planes
above German forests
their trees like Yule logs
glowing, the sky full of silver glass balls.

3   Labour Day

Your mother sings Bing
Crosby tunes, turns bowls of
Bing cherries from her backyard
trees into pies, fills
the vacancy left by
my mother, four-and-twenty
blackbirds
baked inside her brain.
Grandma the tireless
cook who learned her trade
stuffing lumberjacks in her parents' camps.
Flips pancakes on the Coleman stove then
watches you row me out on the lake to where
the rainbows rise, a boy forgets
his father
died too soon to leave
islands of memory.

Grandma married a lumberjack
who learned to fly, went to war,
came back with medals for a wife
inspired by a ladies' magazine
to sketch sailboats on Lake Washington,
mountains beyond Seattle.

After his death, with pen and ink
she drew the dark around
a full and eerie moon,
trees shivering in its light,
and hung it on my birthday
in my room. Your face serene

at the oars, crow's feet
radiating from your eyes
that study our lines
trailing from the stern,
mouth relaxed but teeth biting down
on your pipe, its Cherry Blend
tobacco I try to smoke years later
but find too sweet, liking instead
Balkan Sobranie, its black Turkish
latakia like smouldering stumps
of hemlock, cedar, and fir.

4   Fourth of July

Sparklers. Not firecrackers
which blew out the U of W
quarterback's eye as a child.
We've watched Schloeret, half-blind
evade tacklers and find the open man
in the end zone. We've hugged as if
you've tossed the ball
to where you know I'll be
and I catch everything
you throw my way.

Sparkler batons. I pretend to conduct
Jimi Hendrix's "Star-Spangled Banner"
you think's an insult to everything
America stands for.
Each generation has its war
and this is supposed to be mine.

I'm proud you've worked all your life
at Boeing. Can still hear the clank
of horseshoes you've thrown
at company picnics, hundreds of Boeing
parents cheering our gunny-sack races,
families celebrating inaugural flights

of 707s, the first jumbo jet.
Then, the world changing, giant Boeing
parties in the Kingdome, Bob Hope and
Michael Jackson, smooth white skin
of Cruise missiles on flatbed trucks,
in Canadian skies, the sun's glare
on long-range bombers
trailing white ice in thin blue air.
Hendrix's "Machine Gun" anthem: my
frenzied jitterbug to that.
You and Aunt Fern win the three-legged race
then gulp a gallon of pink lemonade.
Your nephew thrilled, self-righteous,
confused.

Sparklers fly sorties,
fly figure eights, infinity.
Neurons of two brains
fire on the stems in our hands.
We sing the dandelion electric.
Retinas trigger the nerve
to believe we love
to see each other
glowing.

Oklahoma, where the wind comes sweeping o'er the plain ...

Once it was the Russians.
At noon every Wednesday I froze
gaping skyward when the air-raid
siren blared, just testing, but
what better time to attack.
Or when lying face-down
in the school basement hallway
coats over our heads to protect us.

And in biology, Mr McGrath,
who sang the anthem at football games,
listened to his radio then told us
if Kruschev won't turn his ships around
within the hour, Kennedy will command our warships
to fire, and Sherry Payne dropped
the gallon jar of formaldehyde she was
bearing to the dissecting table.

Once the Russians
made the rain in Seattle
spoil our Fourth of July picnic.
Made teenagers pregnant, cities unsafe
with drug-crazed minorities,
law-abiding citizens buy guns,
and the local draft board ask me
how I'd react if Russian soldiers

invaded my home and tried to rape
my girlfriend and mother.
Now, lying face up on my carpet,
I gaze at the screen, the bleeding
bodies and building debris
in a Midwest town, the manhunt
for white male suspects, patriots
with all-American names,

I miss that siren
every Wednesday, testing,
just testing, and the
empty sky.

FOUR WAYS OF DEALING WITH BULLIES

When Jack Tubbs knocked
the schoolbooks from my hand
the fifth time that week, class notes and
laughter strewn in the hallway
I entered the cloister
of Grandfather's smoke-filled room,
armchair facing Gillette's
Friday Night Fights,
to ask his years as a quiet, thin
man, what to do about bullies.
You've got good tennis shoes,
stay in shape, you'll outrun them.
What if they're faster?
They're nothing
but heavy
artillery, keep out of range.
What if they've got a weapon?
It takes real courage
to show them your back,
walk away. All they can do,
shown up like that, is
hurl gutless insults
you won't give one shit about.

Is that why he hoisted
hundred pound bags of
cement on his shoulder
building our patio? Small as
a jockey he wanted to be, back
straight under sacks of potatoes
all day during the Depression,
now just to show me. One Saturday

I sat at his bar, he served me
my usual, cherry Coke with a swizzle-stick
boxer. A customer
drank himself into early afternoon
belligerence, you sonsabitches,
more whiskey, what you starin' at lady,
bartender you goddamn hear me?

Not this time
my grandfather's soft
patient voice, priestly
lean across the bar,
hand on an arm, the customer
floating already toward home
while Grandfather phoned a cab.
He vaulted
over the counter, the stools, and like
saloon keepers in the Western movies
we loved, grabbed the six-foot plus
drunk by the back of his shirt and pants,
danced him to the door and
dumped him outside, slapping his hands together
good riddance. Another Saturday

two cops came in, went with
Grandfather to the storeroom, came out
lips curled back, biting words off
with their teeth, threatening
my grandfather. Aimed his fingers
at their eyes and read them
the law: Get the hell out
you crooks. Backing out
ahead of their badges, they'd demanded
free drinks in exchange for protection.
In twenty years no cops had ever asked,
and Grandfather had always invited them,
a shot of Jack Daniels, in appreciation.
How do you deal with bullies?
He phoned an old friend, the precinct
sergeant, who transferred the cops
to funeral duty. Grandfather's deadpan

reply to the gunmen
after they cleaned out his till and
just before they shot him:
I'll get you. When

Jack Tubbs in woodworking class
pushed me from behind and my head
hit the edge of a table saw,
my hands from my scalp
came away blood, dropped
to a nearby bench and swung up
with a plane, I'll smooth your
rough edges, Tubbs, I'll shave you
within an inch of your life, Jack, it's
Gillette time, hit
the road, man, you run.

THE SANDLOT

I

In the beginning was the wood
and the wood was from God
and God turned the wood into baseball bats
and said, "Kid, get good wood on the ball."

So I was on the sandlot every summer morning
and every schoolday afternoon in good weather.
My station in life: short stop.
Because I loved that word
and the ball kicking up off rocks
into my glove and the double-plays
starting from me to Michael Moises to Lenny Dupree
and the liners I'd dive for into the hole,
ripping the jeans my grandmother would patch once more.
A skinny kid, I had no home-run power,
couldn't bust the windows
of Mrs Gadsby's house down the left-field line.
But I had the eye, drove the ball to the gaps
and stretched almost anything into a double.

So the voice said, "Kid, try out for Little League."
The neighbourhood team was the Italian Club,
Seattle's best, owned by Tomasa's Bakery.
Three hundred kids at try-out day.
Most of us like midget scarecrows
with a cap and glove stuck on.
The coaches tried a dozen kids at once
at each position. A man slapped a score of grounders
to the twelve of us bunched at short.
I was too polite, anxious, confused,
and froze. Not one ball reached me.
Then I got to bat, against the Club's
ace, O'Leary. I'd hit his fastballs
and curves before, on the lot. But now
I was paralyzed by coaches with clipboards,
the line-up of kids behind me, crowds of
fathers urging on their sons.
I took three swings, each a week late,
and a man yelled "Next!" And that was it.
Back to the sandlot, no longer a hotshot
hopeful, just the slickest of the ones
who didn't make the grass,
the uniforms of the Italian Club.

16

II

Thirty years later, Marea del Portilla, Cuba,
I'm with a hundred-plus Canadians at this small
remote resort beside a peasant village.
One day I say to Miguel, "Why don't you
get some villagers together and I'll make up
a Canadian team." He laughs.
Everyone (male, that is)
plays in this baseball-mad country.
Since most of my team never played before
I ask for softball, slow-pitch. Again Miguel
laughs, and scratches his head. Slow
pitch? He finds a softball
in the nearest city, sixty miles away.

On Sunday the Canadians walk down the beach,
through the coconut palms and
at the village, blend with hundreds of Cubans
on bicycles, horseback, and burro-carts
heading for the field. A rhumba band
plays in the tree-shade on a hill.
Palm fronds cover galvanized
tubs full of block-ice and beer.

I'm at short stop, and seeing the ball
off a Cuban's bat, I dive toward the hole,
one-hop the ball and on my knees
fire to the manager
of Kitchener's Baskin-Robbins
who stretches for the out at first.

Our half of the third and an Edmonton doctor
risks her hands to bunt her way on,
loading the bases. I'm up next and
line the first pitch over second base.
Canadians 2, Cubans 0.
It doesn't end that way.

The Cubans have the bases loaded
in the fifth. Miguel pops one
into shallow centre. I back and collide
with a Red Cross instructor from New Brunswick,

two runs score, and then I throw
stupidly and wildly to home.
In their half of the sixth our second baseman,
a broadcaster from Montreal, passes out
with heat stroke. The game is called.

In the bar that night, Cubans and Canadians dancing,
buying each other drinks, Miguel says,
"Ricardo, you make a fine beisebol player."
And I just say, "Gracias, Miguel, muchas gracias."

THE CHEMIST'S WIFE

She was a young chemist's wife
ladling the punch at a private party
celebrating his senior colleague's
Nobel prize. I was awe-struck
of course, and nothing
but her little brother's college roommate
dropped out of school, driving my Volkswagen
from one fear of commitment to another.

There was Bach on the tape deck, then Miles's
Kind of Blue. Stay and talk to me
she said, as if I were big and stable
enough to bond with the complex
molecules in the living rooms.

The prize winner sat in her husband's
favourite chair. Colleagues stood
in the nimbus of the laureate's cigar,
their eyes polishing his large bald dome
for luck. I had backed into
a dining room corner, light years away from
the gravity that locks such men
into orbit around their obsession.

I'm getting drunk, she said, and shouldn't
bore you with my problems. The flowers
printed on her evening dress
leaned into my chest,
brushed against my thighs.
The kitchen was full of wives.

How can he have no self-doubt? she
threw at her husband, or the laureate, both
oblivious. This is what I'll always be,
I thought, a listener,
observing, suspended
between the wall and her breath
and breasts, while over her shoulder

the men achieve
such density they must inevitably
explode, expand into a new
universe named in their honour.

II

JESUS HONEY

I hate the Learneds, everyone's there
for lines on their resumés, and no one
wants sex
                    Remember when
poets got together to drink
and fight and no fucking
feminist poetics
                    What's wrong with
women standing up for themselves
after centuries of
                    Lying down
for a bonk? My brother the stock-
car racer thinks all artists are fags
                    I'm embarrassed to say
I do love the smash-ups, I shouldn't
and God forbid anyone's hurt but
                    It's true, she teases me
for watching Grand Prixes, then looks up
from her book when they crash
all that flying metal, those flames
and fire extinguishers
                    What about sex
at the Learneds, Beth, I didn't know
your husband's a sensual semiologist
                    Stretchers though God
when they come on the track
                    She starts crying
                    All talk, believe me
George is so wrapped up in *langue* and *parole*
he wouldn't know a woman in heat if she
                    Showed him her signifiers
                    Crashing into people
isn't my idea of a rewarding career
                    That's Demolition Derby, not
my brother, he considers race-car
driving an art
                    So he's queer
                    Would you rather have sex
with Jacques Villeneuve or Jacques Derrida?
                    Talk about demolition
those poetry reviews in the *Globe*

What about massage
therapists, Marcia, do they write nasty
reviews and gossip viciously, like she's
a body-works bimbo and he's a shiatsu shithead
                    Oh, no, we're much more
enlightened than all other people
                    Does she massage you
                    Sure, with fuchsia oil
by candlelight, Wyndham Thrill on the stereo
reading aloud from The Orgasm Less Travelled
                    Is "fuck off" a signifier?
                    Jesus, honey
                    Hey, I like that, get me
some Jesus honey. That's what your Learneds need
                    Name your brother's
stock car that. Runs on Jesus Honey. What
an endorsement
                    Jesus Honey Miracle Massage
                    What if Christ had been
a honey-gatherer and we were all jars
filled with golden solar sweetness
no virus could thrive in
and when we die
we're poured in a thick stream
down the throat of the universe
                    My husband
honey of a ham
                    What if Christ had a picnic
instead of a last supper
                    Only men can barbecue, therefore.
                    Has anyone written a bad
review of the bible?
                    Yes, women
I want to write a paper on sexual
slang of stock-car racers for the Learneds
                    And the night sky
would buzz with the light of
billions of bees.

Sarcasm comes easily,
the epigram slashing
your throat, like a chicken
in a Chinese restaurant
two or five years' of work
deboned. My favourite game
as a kid, kneeling on all fours
behind some fool whom my friend
pushed backwards. I work
alone, now, no accomplice
necessary. Watch football,
the tackler blind-siding
the quarterback. Breathtaking.

I don't like this penchant
in myself which insists: if you're nice
you're naive, and I must scratch
your brand-new car with a key.
Yet frankly, most babies
are ugly. Runts
can't be killed but must we
waste kindness, which is
scarcer than talent?
One offhand remark and
the haughtiest girl in high school
stayed home three days
as if I'd broken

her nose. Follow me
home, I'll invite you
off the record
to relax, confide and
play my grand piano then
slam the keyboard cover
on your fingers. Facile,
really. This gift
that makes you
put your head
between your knees
and brace
for the impact.

PREFACE TO A THEORY OF ASSHOLES

We should apply for a grant to categorize the types, prevalence, and self-promotion of assholes.
—C.S. Fine, Clinical Psychologist

We propose to begin our study
with our favourite salutation
to other motorists on the roadways.
Then proceed to the old acquaintance
who phones after a five-year silence
declaring his grief at your brother's
death last year and, by the way, glowing
praise for his friend you're interviewing
for a senior position. Why bother

helping ambitious students, we'll ask,
who buy A+ essays off the internet
then threaten to sue when we talk about
integrity, skills, and honest competition.
We will investigate trust, e.g.,
in the colleague and squash partner
spending the day after your book launch
in the trendiest café downtown
referring to your factual errors
and his superior research you left out;

or your best friend over lunch
forking her tortellini
while you spill your guts
about your bastard husband's affair
with a woman he won't reveal, and cutting
the air with her knife, your friend declares
in her furious sympathy she'll kill
this slimy bitch, then grabs
your bill, squeezing your hand.

We won't ignore mundane behaviour.
Co-workers who never make coffee
and frown at you when the pot's empty.
The man who leaves his pickup truck
running, spewing fumes and fake cowboy
whining through your bedroom window.
The owner of an upscale boutique
who treats you superciliously
until she learns you're not some artist
in your jean jacket and sarong
but the new architect in town.

The man who's built a real
estate empire and rarely tips
you at the restaurant though every meal's
a business expense. We will claim
there are genetic dispositions,
social determinants, and just plain
self-developed assholism. Those who grin
knowingly, taking satisfaction.
Or the enchanters.
Or those who calculate every move,
friendly or gruff, priding themselves
on being politically smooth or tough.
Whatever the pathogenesis

they all display assholistic symptoms.
No one else matters, everything
exists for their leverage and glide
and engagement: the fast lane,
the remote, saliva glands
of politicians, the genitalia
of anyone desirable, the air around
their stereos and their definitive movie
reviews, the videos of their lives
inside their heads we must watch
and listen to with undivided attention.

They have divorced their conscience
the way we scrape off
the grey gummy seal over
lottery ticket numbers.
They deal and we're the marks.

We will ask our control group
how this gift was grafted
to their DNA. We will extend
our parameters to consider if a god
overcome with nausea
at human decency upchucked all over
their souls at birth. If a nightmare
in childhood showed them so withered
and shrunk with regret at an elderly age
they choose to be monster

trucks, to fill with wet cement
and pour it on us, to be steam
rollers and pave us over, their
Autobahn, their toll-free road.

AT WHAT TEMPERATURE

Marsha wants to hide
Milovan's cameras, better yet,
bake them in the oven
with the strudel he wants
fresh every day. Plastic melting
through the house, the door opening
on Milovan's soft body coming
home for sex, emulsifiers
in the dark room, long conversations
in Croatian on the phone, his voice
soothing or hostile and always
unintelligible to Marsha imagining
women or a mountain town
sprawling in the almost violence
of his arms. It is not

the women he endlessly
photographs, not their half nakedness
she later sees in magazines
reeking of the named perfume
or lavishing their skin on designer
fabrics. No. It is the way he works
only in shorts and sandals,
his hairless belly and nipples
holding the eyes of the models who,
Marsha can tell from their poses,
adore him. At what temperature
do lenses explode?

SCHOOLED

When your husband, feminist
that he is,
hauls the dirty clothes
to the laundromat, you come
next door, steaming
like those geysers I
waited for at Yellowstone or
hot springs I could hardly believe
in Iceland. On long weekends

he's too busy
measuring the temperature of
ocean currents, movements
of fish, to rise
with you to the occasion or
even notice you
migrating to other waters.
Weekdays, he bends
over students, computers.

He cooks, vacuums, shops and
earns tenure, almost
an ideal man. He praises your
work as a lab technician, not
everyone can be a scientist, but you
should take night courses, Women's
Lit. or the history of science.
Skipping class, you write
the name of Darwin's

wife on my back
in the shower, trying to wash
all traces of lava from our bodies,
underwater volcanoes
still spewing.

PARIS AND APPLE PIE

Audrey peeling apples.
Audrey's elbow knocks
her grade five students' exercise books
off the kitchen table,
"dammit to hell" splatters the hot
oven air, while Gordon soaks
his painful racquetball feet in a bucket
of ice. This is the breaking
point when
a house collapses around you,
the knife could be slipped
through the ribs and buried, say,
in the flowerbed by the racquet club,
they'd never think to look there
and if they did what satisfaction
when they suspected one of his envious
colleagues or jealous women.

Given the choice of three goddesses
in a party game with friends last week
Gordon said he would
want to sleep with them first
before giving his fruit away.
Audrey weighs in her hand
the rolling pin Gordon gave
for her birthday, purchased in Paris
between presentations, while she went into
early labour the second time.
Oh conferences abroad, said
his face beaming home.
I am three thousand years old,
she thinks, I know how to use
this sword.

REPUTATION

Now there's a taste in your mouth
like the layers of cruddy
linoleum and canned spaghetti
smells in the hallways
outside the rooms you rent
to women and men your secretary calls
"garbage" when I phone to complain
about the bootlegger she snaps back
is your "best tenant"

and when you fall into a rare
deep sleep you dream of a taxi
funky with years of retching
drunks and cigarette burns
and a wire-haired woman with ten
stray cats who tells you Honey
this back seat's our home
sweet home

will you wake up glad
you're old and it's almost over?

Gotta give them some place to live.
Who else puts a roof over their head?
That's what you told one mayor
after another, who knew a good thing.
Derelict buildings for derelicts.
And, with more foresight than all
those smart bastards, you waited for
the demographics to shift, young
professionals into old neighbourhoods,
townhouses, boutiques and cafés on
the once-worthless lots where
your tenements stood.

Remember when you thrived
on pride in your perfect osmosis:
absorbing all insults and threats
with utter indifference?
The snide envy of friends you'd
grown up with. The grudging, squeamish
admiration of other businessmen.

Yesterday one of your slums
burned down. Years ago that meant
gossip, veiled questions in the papers,
maybe a rock through your real estate window.
Now, just the fire inspector's
routine, the owner's name
not even mentioned in print or on air
and the first itch of fear since
childhood appears and refuses
to stop. At your big house
on the bay the antiques and the view
say No one could touch you for decades

but no one could be bothered to now. However
valuable the properties remaining.

but not because the silver-tipped
man in his Lincoln, on cruise control
glares like you're infested
with lice and a virus
that'll crash his accounts.

The grandmother who thinks you'll rape her and
slit her lapdog's throat doesn't faze you.
Or the Ralph Lauren woman in the Lexus who won't
meet your eyes, a bubble of air might
erupt from her mouth, where she feeds with her
beard-stroking husband on the bottom.

Or the high-school girls who grin and wave
speeding by, too bad
you're no hunk in the road dust.
Even so your spirits lift
and are not brought down by guys
at the right age to kill, who hunt only
in packs, throw beer bottles, and yell
"Fuck you, faggot!" Their potency
brief, they will atrophy long before you
stop growing, their arms twisted
by everyone with real power.

You're not discouraged
by Eddie Bauer types in Volvos
offering their sheepskin shrugs,
or golf-shirted brothers, hiphop pounding
from Range Rovers, imperialism
and slavery kept them
off the course four hundred years
and you're a handicap they don't need.

Farmers in pickups,
truckers hauling our worldly goods
don't piss you off, not even
pony-tailed producers in Jaguars
on cellular phones who buy
and sell our addiction to stars and
won't sleep tonight in the airport hotel
because they remember your face like
the last scene in Casablanca.

34

Almost, it's the man with a cross
dangling from his rear-view mirror
who stops and waits while you
run toward his car
then floors it, spitting
gravel and dust in your face.

No, it's the little kids in the back
window of the Winnebago, who first give you
the peace sign, and when you reply,
give you the finger.

VELOCITY

If I go too fast, I runs into somethin. If I go too slow, somethin runs into me.
—Moms Mabley

It starts with a routine
drug stop on the freeway,
a man, unlike you or me
no doubt, well-known to police,
but wedged just as tightly into his life
of pick-up and delivery
as we often are, especially
the weeks leading up to (the) God's
birthday. Law and order

interfere with the ordinary
chaos of traffic, the man's normal
run in the hot commercial
flux. He loses his
cool, reaches under the seat,
floors the gas and clips one cop
with a fender. Gunfire and a bullet
enters below the man's ear, exits
the jaw and his car spurts
into traffic, brain transmitting red
alert to his grip on the wheel.

You're miles ahead, drifting down
the slow lane with your mother
saying she did love your father but
he'd married his job and nothing
helps her hot flashes. Bleeding,

the drug dealer throws the package
out the window, makes himself invisible
at one hundred miles an hour to all except
a dozen patrol cars, four TV-station
helicopters, and three million soap opera
viewers lurched into live, some
not impressed. Your mother's doctor

listens less well, he's tired, and talks
more about grandchildren than medication.
A car passes, way too fast, it's me,
I'm late from my
yoga class and thinking about

last night's dream in which I failed
to show up for my first communion,
instead searching for my childhood
dog, maimed by a car, and
hiding in the John Muir Elementary basement.

One chopper trails away, low on fuel, its
crew "embarrassed" at losing the feed
to competitors. A national network
tunes in. I hear
sirens: in my rear-view mirror an armada
of squad cars behind a speeding
sedan that slams against your slow-moving
Subaru wagon I just passed
and flips.
I don't dare
u-turn to gratify my
fascination you surely don't share, spun
backwards, whiplashed, surrounded
by cops with drawn guns trained on that
upside-down sedan, and helicopters
hovering. My wife used to

believe my inspired excuses
for coming home late. The terms of my
probation also forbid drinks
with female clients. After dinner
watching the news, she will say,
"Did he really think he'd escape" and
"Those poor women, thank God they're
not badly hurt." And there, my car,
live-action-proof, for a moment
part of history, then leaving the scene.

III

BANDAGES

RATIONED

In some countries the water is
rationed, or newsprint, lipstick,
heart repair, gas for the local bus.
The right to ask El Presidente
any question with no fear of losing
everything you've worked for is rationed.
The meanings of words, especially
sacred ones spoken by emissaries of
gods, were once strictly rationed
and no wonder, say the faces on
sarcophagi, starting up at tourists'
babble. Some men
clap down cards and ask why
women dole out sex so
sparingly, yet want more
of what belongs to men.
Holidays for the workers are
rationed, just like chocolate with
kids must be, controlled early
in the war of need and self-denial.
After the war, my mother
came home from the store with
fifteen loaves of bread, twenty quarts of milk
for herself, husband, and infant son.
My father bought a cream-coloured
convertible and two-toned shoes.
Some parents ration how much their
kids can say, they grew up
in the school of hard knocks which were
rationed unfairly. But who said that
champagne or contraceptives,
arable soil, malaria,
voluptuous and satisfied bodies,
a gift for killing at distances, or unshakeable
convictions of righteousness are distributed
fairly? Love is rationed
by everyone. Choosing
what friends to wear, I
withhold and bestow, thinking, you
lovely person, you despicable jerk;
a part of myself I disown
grips the valve as if my heart was
Greenland and one tank of fuel
must last the winter.

Intelligence is rationed,
the kind that makes money
breed like snakes, and that which
raises us above suspicion of
our neighbours, who should want only
what we desire. Tragic accidents
are rationed by invisible
creatures who give the gift of
exquisite pain. Guilt is
rationed, as is awareness
of when one has spit on another's
dignity, and the need to atone. Also
the sorcery of stabbing
people in the back and blaming them
for bleeding on the furniture.
The wounds, the bandages, the friends
sitting all night by your bed
are rationed. The songs
my grandmother sang at night
when she thought I was sleeping.

SAMARIA GORGE

Imagine your family living here
for five thousand years, how many
generations is that, winding
and winding down, from Omalòs Plateau
to the sea. The same ancestral
ground by the same seasonal
river, barely a brook in summer,
then flash-flooding
sixty feet up the cliffs
when the Gorge squeezes tight
through winter rains. Think of your family
climbing fast when clouds descend,

or when armies stir the riverbed's
dust. No one forgets
the paths, up ledge after ledge,
so narrow, so steep, the sun
wedges down, splitting
the shadows. No one forgets
the old caves, how to build fires
unseen by sentries below.
Old women still talk of
the push of birth on goatskins.
Naked breasts and writhing
snakes of their ancestors'
goddess still breeding
on earrings and bracelets.

Envision Apollo, down from the sky,
your family pouring wine
in his temple, while lightning flashes
through the great bull's horns.
Stone houses beneath the caves,
olives and winter figs, goats tamed
from the mountains. The Greeks wanted

much less than the Romans, who flash
and clink as they march,
and herd your men up the slopes
to cut pine trees
they then must float down the Gorge
in winter floods, to Caesar's boats.

The clenched, bruised sleep of slaves
locked at night in the legion's fort,
while the soldiers court your women
at sword point. Empire invincible
until a mightier storm
sweeps it away. The sacrificed
God from the cross.
Worshippers spreading
resurrection cults, your family among
the believers, tearing down
the sun God's temple,
erecting a shrine to their heavenly king.

Think of the next thousand years, Byzantine
churches, icons on candlelit walls.
Soil too sparse for long burials,
bones dug up and washed, entombed
in the ossuary, your family
drinking wine from the skulls
to break any curse the dead put upon them.
And day after day, goat paths and cypress,
brief sunlight, darkness. The curved moon

swords of Saracens, more men hungry
for God, blood, and plunder.
Allah is great, and so is your family's
knowledge of fear, deep as the Gorge,
and the wisdom of hiding—the old caves
always there. Go with your family, again
and again fleeing, mercenaries
from Venice, Turkish knives,
German guns.

And tourists, staring at the small white
church, icons layered with dust, a stone
crypt with a jumble of bones.
Cave mouths inaccessibly high
on the cliffs. Pine trees
spearing the sun.
The Roman fort on a knoll
where I soundly slept, and dreamt
that a woman rubbed my feet with oil.

Disgorged, not from ships
but buses on Omalòs Plateau,
we wind down, knowing only
this barest outline, or nothing
but narrow, and knee-aching steep.
Your family dispersed
to the cities, all this forgotten.
The snake goddess.
Axe head of light.
Paths to the caves.

Soldiers lean on their trucks,
against the shadowed walls of banks,
gift shops, taverna. The cool
way they lean, arms folded,
groin and belt buckle thrust forward.
It is hot, but they seem
not to sweat in their uniforms.
They watch men talk and drink beer
in the plaza, the loose and tight
skirts of young women. And nothing shows
on their faces. Sometimes the sunglasses
follow me, the foreign
flag on my knapsack, as if
they know I've seen films or
read poems by their celebrated
countrymen who should have been
killed once and for all
in the good old days. They were boys
playing soccer. Too much
democracy. But the olive-green
trucks are still parked at this corner
and that, in front of museums, theatres.
As if they wait for the crowds
to come out, this movie to end
and the shameless actress in parliament
turned into marble and smashed
on command. Tourist: take the
guided tour, through the wing
to the right, of Sparta.

STONE HEART

The cypress trees of Crete
grow fast for forty years,
slowly the next two thousand.
The ones that sprout
in clefts of mountains
among small boulders: some grow
around the rock, embrace, even
lift the stone. Centuries
and the rock slowly cracks,
crumbles, leaving a hollow
where villagers hide
icons and heirlooms, daughters'
dowries, and themselves,
from soldiers.
Crawl inside, from the heat, or rain.
You can hear it, still beating.

GATHERING

All day we wade in silvery and dark-green
heat of olive groves
rising and falling on waves of hills.

In olive shoals of barely fluttering
light are old men and women
bending, black crows to the ground

fingers picking, dropping, picking
fruit from black nets under the trees
until their baskets are full

panniers on burros
creak from the strain and the old
men and women go down with the sun.

In America, you say, helicopters
lower over pecan and almond trees
to shake the nuts loose with their rotors.

The grey-green hills go dark at our feet.
Around us, outstretched arms of
trees, some of them older than

Christ. In the distance the lamps
of Agìa Galini, our landlady, eggplant
frying in oil.

GARDENER

Hey, turistas, if I could speak
English, I would make you see
sugar cane dance
to my machete, before this hotel
washed up on this shore
and made the men of Chivirico into leaders
of aerobics, snorkelling guides.

There is much I don't want to learn
but do. That seaweed must be raked
off the beach. That men exist
who cannot move their hips
to the rhumba, and women who
throw baseballs like men.

I know a thing or two
they don't. How to transplant
delicate flowers with the tip of
my blade. The true colours of
a chameleon. Which mangoes are
ripe—I take them around the pool,
ignoring bikinis who
slither for Raphael and Joaquin
with their useless college degrees

and charm. I go to the old folks
scurrying like crabs in
and out of the sun, the honeymoon
couples wrapped like guitar chords
around each other. I hand them
oranges, and the woman writing all day
on the beach, she catches my long throw
with one hand. There is brush to clear—

you see me outside the dining room
windows, inside reflections of Lorenzo
and Joli in their hotel uniforms—
where the garden and the jungle meet,
my arm and machete a metronome
keeping time in paradise.
Here are the scars
where I missed the beat.

Yesterday these newlyweds
traded me their sandals for a pineapple
and the way I slice it—
I live for the sweet
look on their faces
as much as for the flowers singing.

Walking alone on the beach
at dusk, you might see a dark man
come toward you, under the palms,
a long wide knife in my hand
to split the skull
of a coconut for you, its milk
pour on your tongue.

LIFEGUARD

Their first day on a Cuban beach
with their first infant. The playpen
keeps out sand, horse hooves kicking up
fragments of life from the sea.
They quibble over who stays
with the child in the umbrella's shade,
who dives in the underwater light, alone.

The tall black lifeguard walks toward them,
glides as if his muscles are sails.
He does not speak his one word of English
or nod, or meet their eyes, yet
his shadow bends to the crib
and his long supple arms
swing the child above their eyes.
Neither can they speak or move, but watch
as he floats on the sand,
into the sea, waves breaking around his thighs,
the child calm on his breast, under
a mouth that sings to
the whoosh and slap of the surf.

Mother and father transfixed. The sun
snaps its fingers. And running,
hands clasped, they leap at the waves,
letting themselves drift, submerge and be
swept again and again to shore.

I want nothing. I fear nothing. Therefore I am free.
—Inscribed on the tomb of Nikos Kazantzakis

A solitary tomb, a large wooden cross,
the highest hill in Heraklion
bordered by ramparts of Venetian walls,
the symmetry of Mount Ida at sunset
beyond the cross. The church
refused him burial in his city
of birth, his body
placed three times in consecrated ground,
three times dug up. Until one defiant
priest, who'd met the spirit of
God on every passionate and censored page,
found this spot on a rubble-strewn hill.
Now landscaped with lovers, flowering
shrubs, and old couples resting
from the steep climb.

Below the walls, athletes on playing fields,
a maze of crowded tenements, antennas drawing
the light of the world. He is alone
here, like a goatherd, like Odysseus
washed up on the shore. With his own
last temptation, to lift his feet
from stones and nails, and dance
the sun down into the sea and up again
above the mountains. Nothing
now, no guns or fratricides, not even words
between God and his soul.

You say you were lost for hours
trying to find me. No tourist maps,
no signs pointing the way to my bones.
Winding through a Cretan labyrinth
of jammed-together houses and shops,
dodging the bull-headed taxis,
wishing all your words were not useless.
It was not Greek bureaucracy or the priests'
desire to hide me or the soldiers' revenge.
I planned it this way.

You should stare back at the stares
in a hundred doorways, know the faces
I took my disguises from. The beauty of
fiction is that its people don't die.
Especially the murdered.
Down in the streets, they hardly know
the care with which
they were created, or how
painful it was for me to trust
God knew exactly what he was doing.
I breathe easier, even under this stone,
knowing that what passed through me
leaves their throats when they call
their children home from the world
which already has its sights on their hearts.

I am glad you found
that old tunnel under this hill,
walked into the darkness beneath me,
that you were frightened, heard rats
scratching like a prisoner's hand
on his cell. I could see
your eyes when you reached the light,
that field where boys and men play soccer.
Their cries reach me here,
the sounds between times of martyrs and
thugs. And the restless music of the sea
which says: fear nothing, want nothing
and you shall be free.
Go, now. The way you came. And silently
thank those I named,
possessed, drove.

IV

TONGUE PIERCING

There are emergencies
north of the cities
I wasn't trained for, that trick
my brain into hoping
this is a nightmare and not
a nurse's red-blooded voice
pulsing into the phone,
We need you here
now. Even when it's too jesus
late for the young mother and
two small girls
after a truck driver dozed
across the dotted line and
signed them off. I have to
look, verify, talk with the Mounties
about who will call the husband
this time, then face the truck driver's
remorse without screaming.

Or the fifty-five-year-old woman
tonight, sirened from home,
her brain decoding
an overdose I don't know
the nature of, and appalled
at the message, shutting down.
Comatose. Vital signs
slipping. The ambulance ladies
could not get the pill bottle
from her husband, he flatly denied
she was taking anything for her
moods, her silence, her ungodly
display of tears on Sunday at
the Dutch Reformed Church, the only place
he allows her to go
besides K-Mart and Safeway, says
a nurse who knows her.
The pump does its job
but whatever she's swallowed
for years has programmed her brain
to keep hiding, fading away,
and I call the Mounties to bring
him here. He is dumbstruck
when I say, Look,
if she dies, and there's a damn good chance,
it won't be her, or God,

but you to blame. He takes
a prescription bottle from his pocket.
I didn't realize, he says.

Great, it's a drug I know
there's no antidote for
up here. Call Vancouver, yes
they have two vials but
insist it's preferable
to fly her down there.

Somehow, I keep her heart
working, while the plane leaves
CFB Comox. I must deceive
myself into thinking
there's enough strength in my voice
to roll the stone away
from her mind. Frieda,
please hear me, we're tunnelling
as fast as we can, we'll take you to
a place where it's safe
to cry again. The pilot radios
he must turn back
in a near-gale wind and rain, a fishing boat's
adrift in the Strait, the choppers
and divers need the plane's searchlights.

Somehow the air keeps moving
in and out of her lungs, while
the fishermen are found, the plane
refuels. A tired nurse
says, You wouldn't find me
taking the easy way out, and I snap,
Shut up, then apologize.

Near dawn I hold a coffee and
Frieda's hand. So peaceful she
seems, a swami in the corpse pose now,
the yogi's barely detectable breath.
White plantation owners would sleep
with little black boys at their feet
to draw their fever out. Should I
curl my belly
around her soles?

The rescue plane lands.
Others take over.
Frieda, fare
well. I sit down beside
her husband and begin
the morning.

SPARK
      (for Anna Percival, September-November 1993)

Little firefly
we would keep you
a little longer
at least one summer
in the evening yard
grass and branches
lit with your brief fire
the night field beyond our house
and around the veranda
we would keep you
our spark in the darkness
but you were called
by a voice full of flame
to help keep the great lights
burning, in a sky
full of fireflies
so distant, so near

PERFECT CIRCLE
        (for Gerald and Shannon)

The crash in the living room is not
your son, his spaceship circles
a hostile planet upstairs, not his baby
sister with the ten keys of her
hands on your face, unlocked
and floating, a full
moon above her near-sleep.

The crash is the sound you see
as her face twists
the lid off a jar of cries,
your son veers into alien gravity
while you rush by, hammering the steps
down fast but nowhere near the speed of
the hawk that just crashed

through your window. A perfect circle
of languid grainy August air
in the glass, double-pane thick
a gale off the North Atlantic can't crack.
The red-tailed hawk on the smooth
branches of the white pine floor
shakes and shuffles its feathers

like a ballplayer knocked down by a
brush-back pitch, dusting himself off.
Once, flamboyant on the dance floor,
I slipped and flew and landed
on my tailbone: that perfect circle of
silence through which laughter poured.
You don't laugh. An arrow of the sky's

voracity has shot your house in the heart.
The method of release—hawk jumping
on the diaper-changing table,
bath-basin dropped over it,
table wheeled outside—
is acceptable to the outstretched arm
that welcomed it back, message delivered.

GAUNTLET

Conrad goes hunting for geese
once a year, two birds
hanging limp from his farmer's hand,
in the other, a gun
used sparingly, just this.

I stand with him, looking up
at the sky. The silence
that was not there
one hour ago. I'd always thought of

all the geese flying on,
closing ranks on the empty
spaces, the safe passage
beyond *this* field, *this* marsh,
and the long warm winter.

Now I see a man drop
geese on his kitchen table,
lean his gun in a corner
every few miles.

CASTE

1

What a nice country. Riding up
the elevator in a Toronto hotel
well-dressed on business
on holidays and white. Following
dark men who push
luggage carts ahead and we don't
bow they do toward
hands meeting briefly at opposite ends of
five-dollar bills and menus later.
Taxis to meetings and Skydomes with the drivers'
histories packed inside
exotic names on their licenses from Eritrea
Bangladesh or reggae-and-poster-familiar Jamaica.
No time to ask how they think
our future will be different with their great-
grandchildren owning the Gardens the *Globe* the
trucks hauling food and furniture to their outlets
that used to be Loblaws and Eaton's.
Got to get back to the
room to change while
black women hang fresh
towels turn back the covers
leave Ovations on the pillows.

2

We welcome you with open arms. James
from Uganda, walking into my college office
on crutches. Explains. Back home
a student newspaper editor. One day
somebody's soldiers dropped by
and James lucked out
that time, his colleagues filling the space
bullets wanted. Human lightning
does strike the same person twice
and somebody else's soldiers
cut through James's house and left
him wounded underneath
a weight too heavy for God.
His family had shielded him
and so could we, on campus, in Charlottetown,
watch his limp slowly but not quite disappear
as he walked home

one night downtown past Ed's Taxi
where some guys you'd never call "lads"
hung out, spitting, taunting, and
jumped him from behind.

You shouldn't walk downtown alone at night James.
Even women are safer.
So he went with friends to Lord Byron's
live music pub, where students go, and muscle car
men prowling for coeds. This is a nice Island
now, and you shouldn't think
there are more than a few

like Bud Duncan, of the tank tops and
kick boxing and Shania Twain tattoo,
who called James a jungle bunny
pimp and since James wouldn't answer
pushed him off his stool, onto the floor.
James, getting up, called him a coward and
Bud Duncan couldn't see himself
reflected in James's eyes, the soldiers
breaking down doors, didn't hear
in the drums and guitars the automatic
bursts of rifle fire, the groans, the growling
engines lifting James above the Savannah,
away from Uganda, to where
Bud Duncan, ignorant of his own
ancestors, broke a beer bottle
and lunged at James, unharmed,
the local staring dumb at his blood.
James quietly making his statement.

HIKER WITH JAVELIN

Around the headland, wading
through surf, face and torso
tinctured pink by the going
down sun which glints
off the stick
with which he braces
himself against the breakers.

We watch from our campfire
this Neptune, we call him, take
the shock of each wave on his chest;
one roars over his head and splashes
the rock face upright as he
is, below the trail the map says to take
atop that bluff, don't mess with the tides.

Out of the foam, along the shale
he arrives, wet boots and javelin,
slings down his dripping pack,
kneels and takes a mug of coffee
at our welcome. Spreads his gear:
sleeping bag, sweater, twelve cans
of Olympia beer, a hunter's

knife he reverently handles
and each of us holds, imagining
trap lines and a deer's warm pelt,
trout flesh and cedar shavings.
His name, he says, is Eugene
Rosellini. State Governor's last
name, we say—any relation? Yes,

but, unsmiling—Call me
Biff Schultz. Way out here
he lives off shellfish and salmonberries.
Once he bushwhacked through spruce
and salal two miles to an unmapped
lake in November, wanted to stay
and fast until he had a vision.

On the sixteenth day of rain,
motionless in his sleeping
bag, leaf-mould and mud, he wept
and shook uncontrollably. Now
I come to enjoy myself,
he laughs, cracking open
a beer. Unsheltered, covered

in ocean dew he sleeps, and then
while he swims in the sunrisen
sea, I find his
knife, unsheathed
in the sand, half-buried. Ashore, he
takes it back with a two-second grin,
packs up, shakes hands, moves on.

HIS FINAL AFFAIR

I

Blond, he sighs, and a canopy of fragrance
rises from the pineapple boats and champagne
fountain at his son's wedding,
the bride's sister smitten with his sad
eyes, hand glissading in the small of her
back as he guides her
so deeply into the music
outside the ballroom that she lets him
kiss her golden fleece
later in a hotel room while the revellers
grow thick and spent and waxen below.

II

It's her hair
that feels like the small Persian
rug in his grandmother's house
he pressed his ear against and heard
a thousand tales from. Rapunzel
trailing golden cirrus over his head
from his mother's fingers combing
Mozart from piano keys.
The hair he strokes with the same soft
fear when he smoothed the feathers of a sharp-
shinned hawk his father held for banding.

III

Love, he composes on her breasts, is black
volcanic glass, is a fossil in the dried
mud of a sea I once swam in and now
you've uncovered with your fingers
scooping. She unfolds
scraps of paper, each a shining telegram
on the death of his wife.
They placed coins on dead king's eyes
she says, her tongue
piercing his body, she soars
aloft on a column of blood.

At Skeleton Lake

She can smell thunder
not in the charcoal sky, but rippling
out of the lake, bad breath of sunken
trees, their groans in that nastier
darkness. Something quite dead but
still clutching at light, will
seize our canoe, hold it for a white
slash of voltage to fuse our eyes
into slag. Hull and torsos
rocked by the wind. The water knows next
what to do. We stroke hard to shore,
night swinging down on a blacksmith's arm.
She was right: scrawled on the sky
marks of a mad calligrapher.

Inside the cottage the telephone
stutters, a voice that might thrill
the ear with electric fire.
She closes shutters, windows,
blinds, and pulls me down on the bed
and deep inside, when the storm strikes
overhead and surges
along our spines.
We were safer
out there. Limbs on the bottom.
Random chance of one unbearable
instant, glowing. Now
it forks in the bones and
we need each other
to pound on the heart,
breathe again.

GLOSSOLABIA

What am I like down there
she said, and he, kneeling ...

sea foam's
wavy white threads
on the sand

pink morning clouds above
the blossoming pear

the roseate spoonbill
I mean, the small tuft of
feathers on its neck

A Mozart concerto
spiralling down
from the French horn
player's open window

the mouth of that woman
in Agìa Roùmeli, peeling figs
and splitting pomegranates
with her thumbs

a burial on the West Coast Trail
with the ocean's roar and the beads
I stole for a girlfriend's necklace
but buried later
under my dead
grandmother's rhododendron
begging forgiveness

the whorls in soil or snow
of a creature released
from a trap, unharmed

a breach in the city's wall
where light from a sliced-open
moon pours through

I   San Francisco, 1968

The all-night Ocean
Avenue streetcar seemed to run right through
my bedroom. The night after Russia invaded
Czechoslovakia, a long low rumbling,
metallic screech and brilliant flash
woke me to the start of
World War Three. The streetcar's trolleys
jumping the wires. Cynthia slept
soundly beneath the mushroom cloud
I laid awake
preventing. Her nightmares
were different and made her shake
me into half-asleep and frustrated
denials that I had seduced
her best friends Dinah, Mercedes, and Sue.
In my dream, no hope
of survival. Afterward, awake for hours,
memorizing emptiness.
Cynthia filled the night-world with
her meltdown, fallout, and slow
cooling of her core.

II   Hope, BC, 1976

Chuck tells me how the party progressed
after I left. Three couples smoked dope
on the space-out-to-music futon
elevated five feet high on stumps
of Douglas fir. Van Morrison
mumbling. There was Matt the stoned
mason and Fran who read nothing
but Salinger and *Cosmo*, Mordecai the armchair
Marxist and Ruth the macrobiotic woman, macho
tree-planter Sonja and Bruce the nudist Buddhist.
Swaying to music led to massage, which inspired
undressing, which revealed
affinities of appendages
and orifices. Deep and
rapid breathing woke the firs
to memories of winds
aroused, boughs entangled

and the stumps began a rhythmic
rocking, this way and that, leaned
too far and crashed
in a blow-down
crescendo of screams, flailing
limbs, and Tupelo honey.

III   Halifax, 1981

After my professor's wife
removes her silver
tea service, bone
china cups, he fills
his pewter steins with beer,
leads us to their bedroom
to marvel at their cacti
collection. She hangs
back in the doorway like a disapproving
ancestor framed on the wall.
He names succulents
with the same refined lips he
presses to the poetry of courtly love.
Cacti on dressers and nightstands,
crowding the floor. I avoid meeting
his gaze. My master of
poetic irony has lost it
inside his boudoir, and his wife,
obviously bred for handling
collectibles, catches my eyes
and dares me, his protégé,
to touch the thorns.

IV   North Shore, PEI, 1991

Our wedding night at Dalvay Beach
this bedroom is big enough
for the sound of the sea.

V Charlottetown, 1999

You lie in our morning bedroom
as a queen of ancient Crete
lay in her lustral basin.
Sun ricochets off metal
roofs of potato sheds on Water Street
wharves, Irving Oil tankers, ocean liners
funnelling tourists downtown.
You luxuriate in
this hammock of love, strung between
cathedral bells for early mass
and the bootlegger next door
rattling empties onto a truck.
You gave birth last night
in a dream to a sea bird
with luminous white wings and
everlasting life, crying out
its loneliness from sea and sky.

Our cats leave the pool of
light our bed floats in,
quiver their jaws at starlings
jostling for space in the elms.
After my shower, bearing a tray
of coffee and champagne and orange juice,
I stand in Knossos, your royal
consort descending the stairs
to bathe with you in the spilling sun.

PASSED INTO SPIRIT

I want my mother to live forever.
–Lorna Crozier, "Repetitions for My Mother"

I Sleepers

Though we know this must happen
we are incredulous, never prepared
or accepting, and after the mourning,
suspend them in a cryogenic
part of the brain, later to animate
their gentle necessary tyranny, flawed
divinity, their orchestration of craving
and comfort, healing and hurt.
We always knew they'd abandon us, and though
we've learned that's an infantile
fear, no longer viable in sane adults,
try telling that to my very sound friends
who go for walks alone
to talk with the ghosts of their parents ...
so I eavesdrop on conversations
learning how to speak
to my own.

II Wake

One friend's mother calls her son down
from art school in Banff to where
wheat surrounds a farmhouse bed,
a father's voice reaches out
one last time, open-palmed,
no great secret there
except the softness at the dead
centre of so much
impenetrable silence, stubborn
shaping of landscape into history,
children into ventriloquists.

Another friend's father sinks ahead of his son
into blindness. Shuts his eyes the way
he never would the curtains of their
home and corner store, papa's
answer to their neighbours'
suspicion of Jews. The fog
thick over St John's when the son's

plane lands on the eve of the funeral.
He wants to fly the ashes and his own
failing sight to Jerusalem, to say
goodbye forever to his father's
promised land.

On the wet November beach at Spanish Banks,
below her large, stately house on the bluff
with a view that goes on forever,
a mother sets her purse on a drift log,
takes off her heels, unrolls her nylons and
folds them carefully next to her purse and shoes,
sets her wedding ring on the stockings,
her family inside the ring.
Leaving her TV station in Toronto, her daughter
edits the audio, her brother's
call, police report, bystanders' account
into the news clip: her mother walking
across the sand, the shallows,
waist-deep with the gulls, stroking outward
into the riptides and currents.

A mother climbs ahead of her son
on Desolation Mountain, five thousand feet
above Howe Sound, no switchbacks, straight up.
At the top, her son, almost fifty,
spread-eagled, exhausted, sees only
his pulse on the flat blue sky. His mother
sketches wildflowers, tells the birds
their scientific names, practices breathing
in her salutations to the sun. Africa
one month later, she'd wanted to go
after reading Isak Dinesen when young,
Jomo Kenyatta much later. Baobab trees
and giraffes, a lake full of flamingos,
Kikuyu herdsmen and cattle, a tennis court
in Nairobi where she played
with a famous British historian
and died suddenly while
leading four games to one, said the fax
to her son, overcome with what
he could not tell.

And a friend's ancient father
just last month, who'd flown
hundreds of missions over Germany,
and every year flying
whatever small plane the military
loaned him to the family reunion.
This year a farm in Ohio, landing strip
nearby, Pop's last flight because
his balance was shot, hands shook
too much, the military was taking
his privileges and license away.
The family gathered at two o'clock
in the field for Pop's arrival. On time
as always, everyone relieved
he was there, safely, circling above.
He waved his wings then banked
toward Crockett's Hill and as everyone
gasped in shock but my friend
Pop set the hill on fire.

That's how I wish my father had
passed into spirit,
not in a car on the highway
through Tacoma, after three years at war,
wrestling to take control of
the wheel from a drunken pal.

But like Pop, turning the trees the brightest
colours in mid-summer, while his son
amidst all the weeping, waved
and cheered.

I   Privacy

The Plexiglas shield I construct
between myself and fellow passengers.
Their bodice rippers and electronic spread
sheets likewise protecting them
from my serious review of books.
I am no longer enthralled
by the first-time airborne
into rum and running
commentary on why I'd love and hate
their quaint little town. My whole world
becomes a window seat, the porthole
silk-screened with farms, a mountain batik,
wash of clouds, blue oval
mantra Om-ing on.

It's a post-modern cliché: I love to fly,
those precious few hours alone,
work gets done without interruption
in *my own space*, 16A. Not obliged
to care about grandma's trip back home
to Newfoundland, the virtues of
tax cuts or Weight Watchers, or soulful
experiences at Graceland or the Vatican.

Once I craved the slow slide through
small talk toward that zone where being
strangers on a plane could unlock
each other's baggage, out spilled the most
amazing souvenirs, intimate
apparel, stolen goods, trails of cold and
warm blood, and it felt safe
surrendering ourselves
to our voices, the pleasure of one story
in crescendo then yielding to another,
cockpitted against the brief worlds
the plane transcended, insubstantial below.

But the endless busyness of those worlds
intrudes on those of us with urgent vital
work to do: that most impressive
rope round the throat, voice
choked off, neck snapped
back, and listening to the search

76

engines of the brain, ever faster
server, Plexiglas up,
I am, if disturbed, cool and
evil-eyed in my scheduled privacy.

II   Narratives

Descending into Halifax.
The businessman beside me snaps
his briefcase shut. I close my book.
Shields half-down, we ask the usual
polite questions. A broker
of hops, a Dutch master
brewer, living in England
for years, he goes wherever brewmasters
convene, bearing the Wise Men's
fourth gift. Learned and keen

to enlighten, he wants to send me
his monograph on the history of
brewing. I write my name and address
on the back of his business card,
Gerard Lemmens, hop broker. And
genealogist in his spare time,
which I learn while he keeps exclaiming,
as the wheels touch down, my name
in his hand, the lines of
blood, jet turbines roar
down the runway, how close or
distant? Cousin?

This is a first for me. I am one,
though, of hundreds he's met
at reunions, clan Lemmens,
Lemke, Lemm. The mystery and
mutability of my uncommon name
now gone, the guessing game of
origins, my pride in being
a chameleon of unknown ancestors,
inheritor of a dozen different songs
of earth. The Jewish poet insistent
my name and nose hark back
to great-grandfather Lembowski
who fled the pogroms of Poland.
Or boarding the sleeping car

in Montreal and finding my berth
occupied by a Chinese family
named Lem, who stare in disbelief
at this double-booking. And others
claiming me for their own: Felice Lembo
in our football-crazed high school
teaching me about Italian soccer.
And Claudette Lemieux, addicted to Pernod,
George Sand, and two bisexual lovers,
swore I was her Parisian brother
in a previous life.

I've not been to France. My father, though,
fought there. An only child,
born and raised in Montréal,
migrated in the thirties to Seattle
with his mother. Rosie Lemm
survived her son's miraculous
descents on parachute cords
into Normandy and Sicily, his death
by Chevrolet and a friend intoxicated on
peacetime. Twelve years she lasted
into my life, other grandma with my
unusual name; somewhat foreign
giver of savings bonds and a French
clarinet, but no shrapnel
words about her past, the kind that pierce
a child's armour against grownups
reminiscing, fragments
working their sharp-edged way upward
through layers of memory to
break the surface, years later.
Relics from which we reconstruct
those grander stained glass
narratives of our lives.

Rosie, where were your husband's people
from? What devout shtetl, what suffocating
petit bourgeois town, what orders to be
on either end of a Prussian bayonet?

Was there a vineyard, or the skill
of making and playing violins or
shovelling horse shit off cobblestones;
a reputation for strong backs,

cheating on women, boring harangues
over beer, quarrels with God;
or the ghost of a peasant
crushed in the family's mill, who afflicts
only sons of only sons?
And how would such knowledge

change my life? Gerard,
my first in-the-flesh Lemm since Rosie,
after selling hops in Toronto, partied
with three hundred Lemms in Wisconsin.
Tending an orchard of a family trees,
he says I'm a missing branch and
can't wait to graft me onto
where my father ended.

III   Labyrinths

One month later, photocopies arrive
from Gerard. Death certificate
of Matthias Lemm. Born: Minnesota.
Married: Rose Lemm, 1900, Dakota Territory.
Died in Seattle 1936. The document states:
"Children: one: Harvey Matthew Lemm,
killed in a car accident,
no descendants." Broken off at the stem.
Finding this grandfather, I'm not alive,
my father's non-child

staring at a photograph: Matthias
in the "uniform of Spanish American war"–
a Teddy Roosevelt Rough Rider, moustache
and sword, in each hand a revolver, the hero
I long ago wanted a grandfather
to be. From the Rhineland
his family came, from Rotterdam earlier
as sixteenth-century Protestant refugees.
And were you in Cuba, Matthias,
eyes fixed on San Juan Hill, fearing not
Spaniards, but mosquitoes, and bequeathing
to your son the inheritance (he spent
wisely during World War Two)
of watching comrades die, while you,
liberator, went decorated
home? to Dakota? Montreal? Seattle?

Why? and why am I shown your
last-of-the-Old-West face before
the future concealed you?
The best clues are directions
deeper into the labyrinths
our ancestors construct for us.

IV Doors

Gerard writes: many Lemms were religious
fugitives, some Catholics, some Dutch Reformed,
fleeing from Holland to the Rhineland and
Lower Rhine, even Poland, and England
from Flanders. "So you have found
your family again, and what a sizeable
family it is ... because the first
ancestor to the US married 2 times
and each time had 14-16 boys.
Do you have children of your own?"

No, but now I have a family
crest and seal, the "clan" names
circling. Cavalry tents
clustered on a tropical hill.
Groaning wagons, cloaked figures
labouring away from Rotterdam.
Sausage makers in Jackerath, near Cologne.

A man gazing skyward
sees his father's parachute bloom,
his father land safely
in his mother's arms, briefly
but long enough to make him exist,
before the smash of metal and glass.

No 14-16 brothers or sisters
for me. A handsome, two-volume genealogy
and a book, "*Malting and Brewing Science*,
scholarly and readable," writes Gerard.
"You must visit. All the Lemm doors
will open for you, my new friend
met on a plane."